Eyes on Mars

A Poetic Memoir

ALSO BY ROB SMITH

POETRY:
The Immigrant's House
Mzungu, Hello: a Poetic Journal (color chapbook)
256 Zones of Gray

NOVELS:
Children of Light
McGowan's Call
McGowan's Retreat
McGowan's Return
McGowan's Pass
Shrader Marks: Keelhouse
Sand Dollar Island

LITERARY CRITICISM AND COMMENTARY:
Cultural Perspectives on the Bible: A Beginner's Guide
Hogwarts, Narnia, and Middle Earth: Places Upon a Time

TWEEN LITERATURE:
The Spell of Twelve

Eyes on Mars
A Poetic Memoir

Rob Smith

Drinian Press/
Huron, Ohio

Eyes on Mars: A Poetic Memoir
Smith, Robert Bruce

Copyright © 2024 by Robert Bruce Smith. All rights reserved. Except for use in a review, no part of this book may be reproduced or utilized in any form or by any means electronic or mechanical without permission of the author.

Cover design: Drinian Press
Cover photo: Retinal Image

Drinian Press LLC
PO Box 63
Huron, Ohio 44839

Online at www.DrinianPress.com.

Library of Congress Control Number: 2024940411

ISBN 978-1-941929-17-9

Printed in the United States of America

For Leslie, Jeff,

and

in memory of Adam

Eyes on Mars
A Poetic Memoir

Contents

Preface • ix

Eyes on Mars • 3

Funeral Arrangements *short prose* • 7

I Am Still Learning • 9

Night Terrors • 13

Step on a Crack/Break Your Mother's Back • 14

Single Parenting in the Fifties • 16

Saturday Mornings in Youngstown • 18

Behind the Badge *short prose* • 19

Sister • 23

Gifts • 24

Red Huffy • 25

Coffee Virgin • 26

Visitation • 27

Watching • 28

Groundhog • 30

Villanelle for Adam • 31

Sponge Bath • 32

Forest Lawn • 34

Mezuzah • 39

Forecast: Rain Changing to Snow • 40

Kool-Aid • 41

May 4th + Fifty • 42

Covid Recovery • 43

Subtext • 44

Small Town Hand Waving • 45

Entomology 101 • 46

Writer's Lament • 47

Couplets in Time • 48

DNA • 51

Warning • 52

9/11/2001 • 53

I Remember Her Much Taller • 54

Fear • 56

My Last Walk • 58

Tangerines, Easy to Peel • 60

I Didn't Know You • 61

Crispus Attucks • 65

Magnum Opus • 66

Covid Masking • 68

Last Dance • 69

Thanksgiving Parade • 70

Our Birches • 71

Epitaph • 72

About the Author • 73

Acknowledgements • 75

"The real voyage of discovery consists not in seeking new landscapes, but in having new eyes."

- Marcel Proust.

Preface

When my father was my age, he was diagnosed with macular degeneration. His particular form of the disease never suggested a hopeful outcome. He was not one to give up, and for fifteen years he improvised and found ways to live an independent and productive life as a neighbor in his rural mountain community.

On the other hand, my siblings and I have had to add *macular degeneration* to the family histories on file with our eye doctors. Because of that, every year I sit and review a new image of my retina, as my optometrist looks for any changes which could indicate problems.

The fact is that my eyes are aging just like the rest of me, but to-date, my eyesight is fine. That doesn't mean, however, that my vision hasn't been affected by the passage of decades.

I now find myself at the age where I can see my childhood through adult eyes, maybe even my father's eyes.

When we were living those years, my brothers and sister thought our lives fairly normal. (I suppose most children do.) After retirement I was fortunate to reconnect with old classmates who would say things like, "I guess I never knew where you lived when we were in high school."

Comments like that changed my perception of the past. They helped me see how the private realities of life on the ground shaped what my siblings and I became in our adult lives. This was neither good nor bad; it's just the way it was. It was normal.

There was one particular event which changed the trajectory of our household. In the early 1950's we suddenly found ourselves motherless, and distrustful of adult decision-making. When this happened, I was just shy of my fourth birthday. I was the middle child with an eight-year-old sister and a two-year-old younger brother. As the years have unfolded, it's clear that we each adopted different survival strategies to cope with the world, but we were always closely allied in a sort of tribal resistance to decisions made by others, those trying take away the only world we knew.

I have written poetry my entire life. While I have been awarded a national prize, I never wrote to gain recognition. I wrote to give voice to an inner-world of self. Looking over the body of my work shows me how the reality of death has shaped family dynamics, and each person touched by that loss was shaped differently in a parallel setting.

This collection of poems and short prose is a mixture of old and new, and I now view my sixty years of writing with an eye to seeing how it was unconsciously becoming a diary of a childhood journey through trauma and grief. In a sense, my poetry has become a memoir living with childhood loss.

I did a quick search for information on helping children deal with grief. What I found reminded me of the typical counseling model of listening and feedback that I learned in Pastoral Counseling classes at Princeton. One assumption, that is repeated over and over, is that traditional therapy is the first option, even for children. Access to a child psychologist is only an option for people with financial resources. It also focuses on observation and intervention that help can modify outward behaviors.

When our mother died, I was four, my brother was two, and my eight-year-old sister was our only therapist/guide. My father was never one to talk about emotions, but, then again, he was busy trying to earn the money to support a home. He was absolutely clueless about picking out clothes, combing hair, and talking to teachers. When we were little, we wore hand-me-downs from cousins and stressed the grooves in a few hard plastic records that told of the life of Jesus, Johnny Appleseed, and the adventures of Puss in Boots. (By saying *stress*, I mean that the disks even survived our cutting the heads off straight pins to serve as phonograph needles.)

Money was always an issue. When the flow of inherited clothes dried up, my sister learned to hand-sew her school clothes. I always worked, and at sixteen I was being paid minimum wage. With that, I could buy clothes off the clearance rack. It was not unusual for my father to borrow ten or twenty dollars until the end of the month when he would get paid. He always paid me back.

I must confess that there's a voice in my head that still tells me that I don't really need to have the newest or best things. It's better to make-do. This has affected some of my adult relationships. On the other hand, we three kids raised each other by staying unnoticed and living on childish stories which gave us a sense of safety in a world where it felt like there was none to be had.

We created our own security and were not unhappy. In the process we improvised workarounds that kept us together and connected in spite of living very different adult lives.

RBS
June, 2024

Eyes on Mars: A Poetic Memoir

"For we all remember that our childhood, as lived, was immeasurably different from what our elders saw."

-C.S. Lewis,
On Three Ways of Writing for Children

Eyes on Mars

With two images of Mars set
side by side on a screen in front of me,
my optometrist reviews all the planetary features.
I see canals radiating from a central region
which she calls the optic nerve,
but they are that web of canals
sparking romantics to speak of Martians
in flat-bottomed boats
navigating waterways on an angry planet.
I know they paddled fearfully
when life forms were watching from earth.

She points to a dark shadow she called *fovea*
which was so plainly the silhouette of my spacecraft
patterned against the rouge ground,
and I imagine the dust of that place
swirling in vortices of powdery clouds,
blinding, blinding…

"Your macula looks good," she announces,
"Do you take your supplements?"

"I do," I say, "In sickness and in health"
remembering my father's near blindness
when the sands of Mars confounded his vision—
macular degeneration.

"Cataracts aren't an issue, yet," she adds.

Cataracts never haunt my dreams.
This view of Mars looks good to me,
not warlike at all,
and the Red Planet is my friend for another year.

In a dark time, the eye begins to see,
I meet my shadow in the deepening shade;
I hear my echo in the echoing wood—

> Theodore Roethke
> *In a Dark Time*

Funeral Arrangements

My older sister, younger brother, and I were part of the funeral arrangements when our mother died. Being nearly four, I never heard the conversations, but suspect that all the thoughtful adults were living under the illusion that a veil of silence keeps everything normal for those who are really too young to understand.

It was the first day of third grade for my sister who went off to school, but only made it through half the day when she realized that "going to heaven" meant that she would not see our mother again. She was allowed to attend the funeral, but my two-year-old brother and I were spared the emotional trauma.

Somewhere in the arrangement process, someone decided that the best future for the three of us was to be adopted within the family. My brother and I went to stay with an aunt and uncle. They were older than my parents, wanted children, but never had any of their own. My sister went with another of Dad's brothers and his wife. They already had a daughter, and my older sister would be the younger sister.

I do not remember much from those days. It seemed like we were fussed over too much. I remember missing my sister, being curious about my mill-worker uncle's rough Lava hand soap, and wondering when my father would pick us up from this vacation. I was told (much later) that in those days, I would look into the eyes of visiting aunts and ask, "Are you my mother?"

I never did find her. My father broke ranks when he realized that in addition to losing a wife, he had now lost his children. While our Uncle Ollie and Aunt Helen had become my second parents, it was good to go home. My father cooked, cleaned, and supervised a string of housekeepers whose job it was to do light cleaning and be home after school. My sister was in public school. Since our first caregiver was an elderly woman with a heart condition, having two boys loose in the house was out of the question. My father dropped us off at the city Rescue Mission where there was a day-school. After his shift, he'd pick us up on the way home. I remember that quite well. We churned butter once, and I had to sit in the corner because I was not good at naps in the middle of the day. They had some strict rules. For instance, boys were not allowed in a low-gated area which housed a play kitchen and nursery. Once, however, at the end of the day, after the other kids had gone, a kind aide let me play inside. I'm sure I made pancakes which were my father's main go-to supper on weekends when the housekeepers were away.

There was little doubt that my sister was in charge. My Dad could hire the housekeepers, but we could run off the really mean ones in a matter of days. In business-parley terminology, we had an informal management structure. In other words, the people at the top thought they were making all the decisions, but the real arrangements were made on the shop floor. The three of us kept our own counsel, and had our own contingency plans. No adults were ever allowed in on the planning, and we agreed where we'd rendezvous if we ever got the word that our father had died. We knew where we would hide, and we pledged to never again be the victims of funeral arrangements.

Until I went off to college, I shared a room with my brother. "Adam, are you awake?" was one of my earliest questions to the dark. When I said it loudly enough, he always was.

First Published: Rob Smith, *256 Zones of Gray*, Bird Dog Publishing, 2008.
Reprinted: *These Summer Months: Stories from The Late Orphan Project*, Anne Borne (editor), The Backpack Press (14 April 2017)

I Am Still Learning

Some credit Seneca—
others, Michelangelo or Emerson,
but, I say it, too,
still, sounding sweeter in Italian.

Ancora imparo.

Is it a declaration—
or plea?
Matters so little in a dying world.

Socrates claimed swans,
sensing death,
sang more fully and sweetly
than ever before.

I want to sing.
Pushing self into the unknown,
trying the new.

At the end, how little we are—
drifting on a tiny planet
in an expanding universe,
waiting,
perhaps to know as we are known.

MOYERS: Who speaks in metaphors today?

CAMPBELL: All poets. Poetry is a metaphorical language.

—Joseph Campbell, *The Power of Myth*

Night Terrors

On a night when I was seven,
I screamed into the emptiness
of my sleep.
I woke,
heart racing,
mind racing to find myself in space.

I was not alone in the house.

Others were in beds nearby, but
no one came—
no one,
and the emptiness
kept me company
in the darkness.

Step on a Crack/
Break Your Mother's Back

The trek was just over half a mile.
We walked the farthest—
with our ranks swelling as friends
waiting in drives
and on porches joined
our street gang, dangerous only
to wandering beetles on the sidewalk from
Cain Street to Sheridan Elementary.

Don't step on a crack—
with the challenge thrown down,
our leather-soled shoes slapped along the concrete way.

Slap—right foot centered in a slab
Leg stretch
Slap—left foot centered in the next, and we were
grateful for the mason's trowel that edged the pavement
to fit our measured steps.
We needed only to avoid stray twisted fractures
from a tree rooted to lift.

Don't step on a crack.
The words belonged to the game,
not to mothers clad in flowered housecoats,
up early to pack lunches for their shift-bound husbands.

Ashes, ashes, we all fall down
is about the Black Death, or so some say—
another chanted game, nothing to think about,
just words, and ours were never meant to harm backs
or turn mothers' sons toward remorse.

I thought about those words, and
wondered if they meant anything to my friends.
Were they steps of compassion or fear?—
Fear of finding a mommy on the floor?

For me, it was simply skill and step,
the thrill of a run rhythmically spanning a precise distance
until the slap, slap, slap became an airborne,
light tap, tap, tap at running speed
with a last-second twitch left or right
to avoid a jagged break.
No cracks under my feet!

A day came when bravery, delinquency, and anger
ran together and I dared a new footfall.

Step on a crack!

Slap—right foot on a seam.

Break your mother's back!

Slap—left foot on a seam.
Tap, tap, toe-tap on each crack
in a spidery soup of broken pavement.

My sister shrieked as if I had dealt a cruel blow,
but what was a broken back to a woman
no longer in memory and long underground?
Wasn't she beyond hurt?

The game stopped.

I could avoid the cracks.
I could *hit* the cracks.
I just couldn't win.

Single Parenting in the Fifties

Half my Father's wages paid a housekeeper,
someone to be home when the three of us walked back from
    school.
Part of the deal was room and board during the school week,
and she had the first floor bedroom—
the four of us in the attic.

Most didn't last long in the revolving door of childcare—
we being the default excuse—though striving to be good—
not wanting to add to a father's despair.

Some lasted longer:
Winkie was my sister's favorite,
nineteen and pretty—
but my father was troubled one Thursday
when he had to work overtime.

Thursday evening was her church time—
she bundled us up for the meeting at the Kingdom Hall.
That evening still lives in my head—
sitting on folding chairs in a large room.
A girl my sister's age stood up to do a reading,
just like a grown-up.

It felt like a safe place.

Soon after, Winkie was gone.
We never asked—no one ever explained—
but a child's mind weaves its own reasons.
Her husband was in prison for refusing Korea—
but that couldn't have been a reason.
Dad's nephew spent World War II in Leavenworth—
He was raised a Witness; never fully employed after release.
Many years later, he told me that he loved my mother—
she was the only one who welcomed him back.

I envied his memory of her.

Gray-haired Mary liked having my brother and me
sitting on her lap, and pressed us against her ample breasts.
Her adult son, Malcolm, always took my little brother to the
    basement to shoot an air rifle.
In later years, my sister called her abusive—
we thought it love.

For a short time, we had another—
but I can't remember a name.
She called me in from the vacant lot next door
(adults never got mad if you stayed outside)
but it was time for afternoon kindergarten—
she gave me a short-sleeved, white dress shirt on a hanger—
perfectly pressed.
That had never happened before—I loved her.
She taught my sister to sew with small stitches,
but she lasted a short time—
her boyfriend came to visit one day,
and left with all our bed sheets.
Daddy couldn't afford to buy new ones.

Saturday Mornings in Youngstown

Shaking and humming under the rubberized whir of traffic,
the steel grate decking of the Market Street Viaduct
terrorized my sister.
She was sure each step would be one step closer
to our falling through the grid.

Week after week, she faced fear
bravery rewarded—
each of us keeping the nickel
our father thought would tinkle to the bottom of
a spring-beveled glass box on some city bus.

Google Earth measures the route at two-and-a-half miles,
but, in those days, distances stretched longer
on short legs from our house
near the water tower on Indianola
to junior choir at our church downtown.
The tower became our homeward beacon,
and the bridge, the dangerous, downward slide into the city.
Beneath our feet ran a caramel ribbon we called Mahoning
winding its way along rows of sooted sheds,
dwarfed by smokestacks belching wages
from furnaces never extinguished,
until they were.

I was almost eight, but too little for handbells,
so Donny Patrone and I would sneak away to Woolworth's
where five cents became a fountain coke with two straws.
Once when walking back to the church,
I saw my Great-grandfather sitting on a bench
with other old men.
Not waiting for a bus, just waiting.

BEHIND THE BADGE

When I was little I wore the badge, but just a pretend one. My favorite was a tin deputy's badge. The Lone Ranger had a five-pointed star of Texas. Jack Webb had the shield of the Los Angeles City Police. Even in black and white, I knew those were real, and the men wearing them were serious crime fighters.

Sixth-grade boys at Sheridan Elementary wore badges. They were the crossing guards on Hudson Avenue. Their shields rode on white fabric belts hugging waists and looping over shoulders, a woven strap like General Pershing wore in the photos from my Dad's books about the Aero Squadrons of World War I. The Hudson Avenue Boys, however, weren't pictures. They wore real safety patrol badges. To me it seemed that any boy who wore that badge was *somebody*.

In fourth grade, I became the boy behind the badge, an unexpected bonus coming from our principal, Mr. Brooks. It began when Miss Jann said that fourth, fifth, and sixth graders were taking a trip to Isaly's Dairy Farm. Only two things were needed: a signed permission slip and twenty-five cents for lunch and ice cream.

That was a problem. I could get permission, but twenty-five cents? I couldn't get hold of that kind of money. I didn't have it, nor did my sister or brother. I didn't have any loose teeth; and my Uncle Wilson wouldn't come from New York until summer. We called him our "rich" uncle. During his visit he would shake our hand, and a half-dollar would be in our palm when he let go. As an eight-year-old, I did the only honorable thing. I told Miss Jann that I wasn't allowed to go on the trip. She understood. The pressure was off. That's when the principal talked with us.

I say "us" because there were five who didn't have quarters. Mr. Brooks called us to Mrs. Perkins' room to explain. Her room had been home to me a year earlier. She had a divided class, half the room was third grade and half fourth grade. When she was teaching the fourth graders, we were to read. A shelf of National Geographic's was right next to my desk with all sorts of educational pictures. But, this day Mr. Brooks called us for another reason.

With sixth graders away, he needed crossing guards for the lower grades. If I was hearing right, I would be behind the badge! It got better. The school had no buses; we all walked. The school also had no cafeteria, so we walked home and back at lunchtime every day. Mr. Brooks explained we had to be at our places before the earliest returning students, so we would be allowed to bring lunch to school.

"Unless you live close by," he said.

I didn't live close by. The boys whose backyard bordered ours went to Fosterville the next neighborhood over. We lived on the edge of the district.

"I live pretty far away," I said.

"How many blocks?"

I'd never thought about how many blocks. We walked down Cain to Hylda, turned right on Hudson—the school was on Hudson. We walked on three different streets, so I said, "Three."

"That's not very far," he said.

Then it occurred to me that "blocks" weren't the same as "streets," so in my mind, I started walking the route and counted each place where we crossed streets. Seven! I didn't report this to Mr. Brooks, but I knew two things: I was going to eat lunch at school, and I was going to wear a real badge.

That day I carried a grocery bag that held an apple and a bologna sandwich wrapped in wax paper. When everyone left for the dairy farm, I was alone in the room. The teacher left some activity pages and drawing paper. My main job was to not get in trouble. When I think back, I wonder why they didn't put us into one room, but then five boys in one place might be more trouble than one in each of five places. Every once in a while a teacher appeared at the door. All the rooms of the upper grades were on the second floor. It was very quiet.

Before the lunch bell, we met for what was the safety patrol's equivalent to matadors preparing to face the bulls in the ring. The canvas strap had to be cinched down to fit, but there was no mistaking the badge. Under the silver eagle at its center was the word "Lieutenant." The eagle was on a field of red. I'd have preferred blue, but it was a real badge.

I wished I was taller.

It was drizzling, so I donned a yellow slicker which, like everything else, was too big. Finally, we were armed with lances. Okay, they weren't lances; they were wood dowels with flags that said, "Stop."

We gathered in the squad room. I had my sandwich and a cup of water from the drinking fountain. I saved the apple, and soon we were at our posts as the lower grades returned. I wondered if they thought that I looked like one of the regulars, the real safety patrol.

I wished I was taller.

I discharged my duty, returned my badge, and went back to the room. I wondered if I should tell my friends about the badge. They arrived before the final bell, the guys buzzing about everything they had seen. I thought ice cream would be the big deal, but they saw cows connected to machines that drew the milk across the barn through transparent pipes. One of the boys found a cow horn that had been sawn off. And he was allowed to keep it! This was hard to believe. They swore it was true, but I wasn't sure.

When I walked home with Janet Lightbody, she said it was true, and she wouldn't have lied.

"Could you really see milk running through pipes?" I asked.

Sister

When mother went away
to care for the baby,
sister took charge.
It was the way it had to be
with little brothers, and
mother being so soon
gone.
Father was busy
working numbers,
but seeing only dead ends.
Strong children rise
to needs unspoken knowing
that at the center of a house is a place
to run when dreams
turn dark,
or teacher says "Everyone, remember
to take your pictures home,
the ones you made for your mothers."
Such a simple thing,
but she went away to care for the baby never seen,
and school art was loaded into a dresser drawer
till sister would bring out her
drawings to lay
side by side
in a children's gallery
seen by no adult eyes.
It was the best she could arrange.
It was the way it had to be
with mother so far away.

Gifts

I still see my great-grandfather, on a bench near Woolworth's.
Seventy-three when he first held me,
an old man walking the front edge of my life.

On another day, he'd be at the break in our fence.
No telling how long he'd been watching
from the place where his hives used to stand.

We'd be all "Ollie Ollie in free" until someone cried,
    "Poppy,"
and we'd turn to the little man who knew the secrets
of electricity and bees, pigeons and dynamite.

He'd give pennies that he ought to have kept and
never would come up to the house, we didn't know why–
waving us off with a faraway glance homeward.

His wife died there, in our house–
his granddaughter caring for them.
She was dead, too, and later, my father would be upset
about the pennies that we had taken.

Older now, I understand
how the music of our shouts
made his old bones human again.

Then there was a visit to the boarding house–
the rented room where he lived.
It was dark and smelled of the incontinence that always
    followed him.

A hotplate lived on a small table near
a jar of pennies proudly poured out
as my Dad slipped a dollar under a soiled doily on the dresser.

Red Huffy

Pedaling with fury
of wheeling sprocket
racing downhill
adding muscle
to accelerating
free fall,
then standing
full height
levitating on pedals
above the earth,
hot air rising from
freshly rolled asphalt
becoming hot wind
rushing over
arms outstretched
in balance
without grip.
I am become
the cyclist
who invented flight.
My brother
only watches with envy
as my red Huffy
blurs in a jetting
streak of imagination.

COFFEE VIRGIN

Tea was the hot drink at our house when I was young.
I smelled the coffee at a friend's down the street,
and Uncle Ollie took a thermos daily to the Sheet and Tube,
but, at home, we were all tea with milk and sugar–
as grandma made in pots with cozies–
poured out with biscuits and her Scottish burr.
My father thought it typically American,
but then, he grew up thinking *stovies* was *goulash*
and pipers in the parlor were ordinary
when sisters were dancing.

I first drank coffee at a hospital,
working there in high school,
filling the aluminum pot to the designated scum line,
keeping it hot over a Bunsen burner.
In those days,
Starbuck was still first mate on the *Pequod*,
and coffee was good to the last drop,
while at the lab, we faked the campfire boil/burn
that Doctor Nelson liked.
"It'll rust your pipes," I was warned,
but my current physician pronounces it healthy.
I trust her, and savor my daily medicine
in a mug drawn from a carafe washed only for company,
and tasting unfancy and delicious to the end
as I had learned with strangers becoming friends.

VISITATION

A boy, a man;
A boy and his father hand in hand
Crossed a field of fresh cut grass,
A quiet place, a home of the dead.
They stopped, then stopped again,
And came, at last, to a marker, a home, a bed.

The man bent down to read the name
"My Dear," he whispered, "Here is your son."
And the little boy cried, not for his lost mother
But for his father in this moment of loneliness.

And now as a man I returned to this spot,
Where now the one grave is not alone,
And I prayed that at last these two graves were one.
And the little boy cried.

NOTE: This is my first published poem. It appeared in the 1965 edition of *Dimensions*, a high school literary magazine. A classmate on the editorial staff congratulated me on its inclusion, but immediately followed with a grimace adding, "It was all about death."

Watching

Bill had a watch
and an airplane made out of a white bull's horn.
The watch in his pocket,
the plane in a corner cupboard
behind glass shutters
where a boy could not reach.

Bill was a mystery,
my Gammy's husband with my last name,
but not a grandfather.
Gammy said his real name was Polish,
but took the name "Smith."
More American, he thought.

My Grandpa Smith
came from Glasgow
and called the name "Scottish."
He was always a stranger,
probably a watch in his pocket, too
but buried before my father was nine.

Bill's watch was not gone.
It came out like
a magic talisman,
always a delight
at the end of a chain.
Beneath the shiny cover,
a white face with crisp black features,
X, V, and I's.

For years I wore a watch on a wrist
shackled to time.
Now, like a smooth stone,
time lives in my pocket.
I open it
and look into its eye,
not to see it,
but to be connected,
to Bill, to Gammy,
to a bull's horn that looked like
it might fly.

Groundhog

There was a groundhog on the trail,
dead,
without any visible marks,
still.
The road runs so close
he could have been bluntly struck
only to race this far,
not knowing the death he carried
in his body.
Knowing, he might have preferred
to die here in a place of solitude
without fume
waiting for me to walk by.

Maybe my imagination plays tricks
and he came gently to this
spot to sleep,
stepping out of his body
as a friend of death
recognizing what
he and I have always carried in our bodies
and taking the lighter path.

Villanelle for Adam

Still, he is this little brother of mine,
who, in early days, was easily caught
when running such games as brothers will find.

Imagination always drew his mind
in the long hours he was lost in thought
still, he was this little brother of mine.

And yet, there were contests in our time,
baseball and kickball where tempers ran hot
when running such games as brothers will find.

At night, when awake, we could share our mind
whispering the secrets our kinship brought
still, he was this little brother of mine.

With light came school and chores and work in kind,
but always, home again and comfort sought
when running such games as brothers will find.

So now, he lies close to death and we bind
the many long years lived so far apart
still, he is this little brother of mine,
and we run such games as brothers will find.

Sponge Bath

Even if bathwater passes
an elbow dunk test,
a wriggling, soapy,
little piggy-guy
defies grip.

When my little brother arrived,
I'm sure I watched my mother
in a washbasin balancing act—
juggling pure-floating soap,
a towel, and a dry diaper—
all disappearing into a puffy cloud
of baby powder.

I would like that memory,
but I was two and can't recall
any bucketed bath—or her.

I do remember—years later,
when the hospice nurse took away
the catheter and the hanging bag
pouring fresh, bubbly-clean froth
into a basin.

The washcloth came to me,
and I scoured away the last
detritus of life from my little brother,
who didn't slide away
or giggle or shiver
as I dipped the terrycloth into the slosh—
fisting away the gushing excess
of tepid water to rinse his cooling limbs.

The nurse had no words,
but I thought of two orphaned boys
plopped into a tub,
one in front of the other,
and a quick "About-face,"
taking turns washing play-encrusted backs.

Tonight, he doesn't twist or slip,
and I send him off in a hearse
with people who will never know.

Forest Lawn

Yesterday, I stood on my grave
raking winter's fallen twigs
acorns jumping
between the wire tangs
of my rake.
My little brother
listened in silence to my monologue,
a comedic litany of all his usual complaints
about this place.
He'd never want to be
near "that park,"
certainly not next to "crazy Aunt Dorothy."

I was once told that you knew that you were
Appalachian if you knew where you'd be buried.

"Adam, do you remember–
twice you stopped me
when I pronounced the word like a native–
You learned it in Tennessee
and agreed I had it right–
Appa-LATCH-un
NEVER
Appa-LAY-shun?"

I didn't listen for his response.
I just loaded my bucket
to take the last
of the shards to the brush
piled near the ravine.

"Remember you insisted on
ashes scattered at the Cleveland Zoo?
Wasn't safe there—been bulldozed for a new pavilion.
Better here."

Don't know if he heard
that last bit,
but I told him
I'd be back.

Either the Darkness alters—
Or something in the sight
Adjusts itself to Midnight—
And Life steps almost straight

        Emily Dickinson,
        We grow accustomed to the Dark—

Mezuzah

A brass mezuzah
clings to my doorpost
with star and numerals
hovering over blue-green metal
feigning antiquity.

Inside—a scroll,
a scrap of rolled ink declaring,
in a font too small—read right to left,
a voice on the edge of silence.

Its case is small and easy to ignore
hanging there in muted tones,
like the trademark of a sash company
guaranteeing tempered glass and storm protection.
But the sun's rising taps it awake.
Before my fingers touch, it burns with memory
of how copper and zinc are transformed,
crystallized and annealed in the fire of its creation.
Something in me believes this is not a trick of the sun,
but the wisdom of the *klaf* rolled so tightly inside,
its script blazing in words beneath my fingers
reminding me of all beginnings.

Forecast: Rain Changing to Snow

Water slides ahead of the blade,
the vanguard of translucent ooze
beneath the camouflaging whiteness
that has yet to decide its species,
snow or rain.

The children two houses over
are shouting
their verdict in laughter
as if this were the first winter
they'd ever known.
They carry no shovels,
and do not know the dangers of slush freezing hard
beneath a sugary white crust.

This is not the first snow,
it's the change that cheats the pavement
of the last of the sun's warmth.
And now, I side with the change,
pushing slush that will soon be ice,
regarding the future
less than the journey,
and the shadows of the valley
less than the hot coffee
and the heat
on the other side of the kitchen door.

Kool-Aid

My wife and I started keeping to ourselves,
after all, there was Covid-19,
and she had taken epidemiology.
I've buried hundreds, maybe a thousand.
I've lost count.
Friends told us that it was all for nothing,
that we drank the Kool-Aid.

I have been to Guyana, to Georgetown.
Fingers, my taxi driver, said to stay inside the compound,
where my skin wouldn't give me away,
but I went out, right there
in that land where Jim Jones actually served up his punch,
his own and other bodies left bloating in the Caribbean sun,
American bodies.

There are worse things than dying.
Killing is worse than dying.

In Guyana, they close the dikes at high tide because
the city would flood like clockwork with the ocean's rising.
Knee deep, a woman with elephantiasis is waiting for a bus,
her swollen leg tells me of the microfilarial worms
living in her skin,
just like the pictures from *Invertebrate Biology* in college.

It upsets me that they say, "You drank the Kool-Aid."
I didn't.
They haven't yet seen,
They just don't know.

May 4th + Fifty

In 1970, I was living in New Jersey,
knew of Kent State,
though not any state named *Kent*.
For me, it was a college,
one I might have attended
years earlier,
except for a small school
in a sleepy town
that better served a scared
seventeen year old,
still new to the world.

In 1970, I was a different person,
graduate of college,
a master's candidate at Princeton—
still driving a truck on the days I had no classes—
maybe just a blue collar among the bluebloods.
Not really alone, though.
John Munson was a bow hunter from Iowa,
Hak Jin-hyung was from Seoul,
both seekers
(not the Harry Potter kind),
but trying to make sense of the idea that
God is Love, yet knowing
people like us
were being shot in Ohio.

Covid Recovery

Potatoes sense the change of season,
ours sprouting in the lazy Susan
as spring approaches, and
I wonder what *didn't* Susan do
that made everyone call her *lazy*?

On that carousel of captive groceries,
the spuds whisper in the darkness—
plotting the breakout
from the netted bag where they live
in the back of the cupboard,
a shadowy hiding place
among half-empty cereal boxes
in the twilight of laziness.

I wait in the same dusky lockup,
eyes adjusting to the dimming light
of this day-by-day spinning marble,
wondering if *normal* can ever follow
virus-choked in the dictionary,
or anywhere else.
My hopes turn to taters plotting—
feeling for light with spiky white tentacles
reaching, reaching, reaching…
as I strain to hear the softly muttered hope
of an old potato sprouting.

Subtext

The driver ahead of me is texting.
I can tell by the way he puts his head down
as the car swings to the berm.
Then he's all head-up with
a jerk to the dashes between lanes.
I am distracted, too
by him,
and by memory of a funeral,
a double funeral
mother and daughter on Route 7
coming home from their shift on Brown's Island.
A semi disrespected the little car they were in.
They were tired, but not texting in 1976
and now they are together in one casket,
the funeral director explaining that it was
too hard to separate the parts,
the family thinking a single closed box
fit them as well as their sub-compact.

His tires roll into the rumble strip
along the shoulder and he startles.
For a moment he pays attention.
I rev up to pass
and my wife is still asleep next to me in
our little car.

Small Town Hand-Waving

Big city friends would find it bizarre,
that I'll wave at any passing car
even if the window's reflective glare
will keep me from knowing anyone there.

As it passes, I may see
a neighbor's hand waving at me,
and, if not, some stranger's confusion
at what is not a familiar reunion.

With cars so much alike, I fear,
the problem becomes very clear:
A Honda or Prius
might be a Ford or a Kia,

I'm just saying that, in the main,
most pickups look nearly the same.
So the stranger has to pass as a friend–
which is as they could be in the end.

Entomology 101:

Aphids are sucking insects that feed on the sap of plants and secrete a substance called honeydew. This sticky resin is a favorite food of ants who actually "milk" the aphids. This relationship is symbiotic, both receiving benefit from the arrangement. The aphids provide food for the ants, and the ants protect the aphids from predators like lacewings and ladybugs.

A whole world
exists under a leaf
on my window sill
where some aphids live,
 all clustered in quiet desperation.
Fear makes them restless,
as they toss in a troubled sleep.
Mostly, they worry that ants
will soon return through a hole in the screen.
They'll come like pickpockets,
deftly touching and
stroking swollen abdomens
drawing out the honeydew.
Ants are the enemies—all hands and legs,
moving so nimbly—smelling of formic acid
and so alien.
The aphids bear up by counting small blessings.
They credit their prayers
with deliverance from lacewings and ladybugs,
and, now they pray only for peace—
peace from the visitation of marauding ants—
peace in their world
on the underside of a leaf.

Writer's Lament

I've declared war on hawthorn,
the tree—
not the writer who shook hands with Lincoln,
and commiserated with Melville.
My hawthorn grudge
emerges under the fence
where I never planted;
it comes unasked and unwanted
from ancient rootstalk
undeterred by my hacking,
as unrepentant as Hester Prynne
and making me the guilty minister
who fears what living stems
do to cedar boards
stretched on a scaffold of
pressure-treated two-by-fours.

Nathaniel hasn't commented,
but he's been out of touch
and few know his work
unless assigned by a teacher.
(NOTE TO STUDENTS:
Wikipedia offers a summary,
but kill the hyperlinks when
cutting and pasting.)
Cutting never works.
The stems come back from those
sons-of-dirt roots that want a
hawthorn remembered,
even if pruned of its silent e.

Couplets in Time

When I was young, it seemed to me,
that years' advancing would set me free.
Sixteen came and I drove a car,
but with wallet so thin— not very far.

In marriage with children, I didn't fare better,
there were bills to pay and inclement weather
with a roof needing fixing, and the car, a muffler
(when I say it like this it sounds like I suffered).

Fact is, old age brings more dreaded demands:
"Come in!" "Go out!" all persistent commands.
You'd think I'd adjust to each syllabic blat
that becomes the life of one owned by a cat.

EMILY. Do any human beings ever realize life while they live it—every, every minute?

STAGE MANAGER. No— Saints and poets maybe—they do some.

-Thornton Wilder
Our Town, Act III

DNA

I am American,
grandparents coming in boats,
my father's on Scottish
steamships with printed menus
from quayside docks on the river Clyde.
My mother's—less known,
still American—maybe more.
On a day, or month, or year—
walking to the Atlantic shore
naming themselves Wampanoag,
People of the First Light,
which they saw coming on eastern horizons,
where they fed pilgrims,
(some free, some indentured)
and Africans who came
in boats not named as flowers,
who did not walk the decks
being chained with other chattel
 waiting for First Light on a foreign shore.
So here I am,
a child of Scotland,
offspring of pilgrims and slaves
Algonquian-speaking, West African, European.
I am American.

Warning

Our peach tree rues an early spring
though reddening finches choose to sing
and whiteness melts through warming haze
'til earth is clear of bite and sting.

But the warm nights and warmer days
seduce unwary stems to sway
in Bacchanalian pleasures which
in leafy green will tease out May.

Yet, March is cruel to those who rush
and April, yet may send the crush
on all intemperate dreaming.
The orchard speaks with petaled blush

against all rants and screaming,
frosty bones and frozen scheming.
When spring comes without careening,
weighted boughs are all redeeming.

9/11/2001

One day they went to work
and didn't come home—
becoming, instead
a point in someone else's argument.
They were thinking of mortgages,
airport connections,
and braces on kids' teeth,
when trapped by other ideas for that day.

Ideas are not people
but they can fly planes,
so sisters and brothers with different dreams
don't come home.

But, ideas can also fly without planes
landing in places of hope and aspiration—
ideas in their own right,
making the argument for a world
where lambs and lions lie together
and people come home from work.

I Remember Her Much Taller

I remember her much taller than she was.
Of course, I was only six
and everyone was tall
except my little brother.
In the pantry was a calendar with a beautiful princess
crowned with tiara
face framed with rosy cheeks,
but no longer a princess,
Elizabeth, her royal highness.
My grandmother was Elizabeth, too,
her only claim to royalty,
a sister, a cook's assistant at Balmoral.
At Grandma's house
another form of nurture reigned.
To lost boys came
biscuits from brightly colored tins,
white tea, and buttery shortbreads.

The kitchen was bright and sunny
on the second floor.
In the hall,
a picture of a Sunday school class, my class.
I remember the day it was taken,
and why I sat
so angelically—next to teacher
while others
played to the camera or ran amok.
Donnie, Billy, Glen, and Wendy
the names of childhood friends
nearly gone from memory.

My mother dressed me for that picture,
not without protest,
wearing white shirt, bowtie,
open jacket, short pants,
and Buster Browns.

I hated wearing shorts.
Men did not wear them,
why should I at four?
I didn't want my picture taken,
knees bared in so unmanly a way.
I sat by the teacher,
out of center.
"Out," teacher said, "of the camera's eye."
She had lied in church that day,
the day I sat on the outside of my own world
and watched children being children
while I sat as a man,
bare-kneed and alone.
I don't know if my mother ever saw the photo.
In time, it came to define me in the Grandma world,
but so did the biscuits and tea
and the wey
she sang tae us,
"Lizbeth."

Fear

As a child
I did not appreciate fear.
Oh, there were
baby fears
of dark basements
haunted by hulking
furnaces with
long arms of gravity-fed
cold air returns.
They were just pipes
and shadows.
They did not hit like the Toughs
who thought me a small, safe target.
Only twice did
any land the stinging blow.
I remember their reactions,
both the same,
though years apart.
I must not have done it right,
not to suit them.
After straight shot to face,
they stopped
heads turning to silent companions,
as if their attempt at improvisation
had left the story-line.
I failed the audition.
Was I to fall?
or cry?
or run?
Like an idiot,

I did nothing.

They should have told me.
I just stood my ground
and they wondered if I had
seen the stars.

I had, but not enough to appreciate fear.

No second punch ever found me,
and the two traced
wide circles around me after that
as if I knew the secret of
their souls,
the boy who didn't
fall,
or fight,
or run.
In time, fear found me.
I see the ones I love
at a distance
where fate makes helpless.
Easier to take the blow
and stand-down
the bully.

My Last Walk

My last walk takes me along the highway,
a path so straight no four-legged creature would forge.
Nothing more than a train bed stripped of rail and tie,
trying to go wild.

Traffic floods my ears,
but not my eyes.
Walls of tree and shrub
rise towering left and right
like Charlton Heston at the Red Sea,
not Moses at the *yam suph*,
an adventure without special effects.

This path is becoming real
with howling wind and shaking boughs.
Birds gone to cover flushed at my approach,
but this is their place now.
I, the invader, who did not come to conquer.

A trail of lasts,
last blue chicory staring up from swirling leaves,
last of the sumacs' red foliage with
cone-shaped parapets guarding the flank,
monarchs too weak for Mexico looking for
the last of the milkweed.
And the berries of white and blue and red,
Dogwood, grapes, haw, and a fruit
so red-ripe a grownup would warn against tasting.
Boys deserve such warnings,
fears grow slower than feet.

These last grapes were small
too bitter, I thought, but still, I tasted
sour and mostly seed from a summer beyond dry.
A boy would eat them,
one who had sworn a childhood oath to run away.
The clan would never be broken.
We would escape to the woods
eating berries and fruits like woodland tribes.

These last fruits belong to others now,
to birds lying hunkered in the bushes,
the worst eaten last,
fruit for desperation of a spring delayed.

Tangerines, Easy to Peel

Tangerines, easy to peel,
yielding to little fingers
as if the pungent rind could not bear
the soft touch of the fruit.
Always leaping free
at first puncture of dimpled end.
It was orange, but not orange,
with sections that fooled only
eye, not mouth.
Dry and sweet without the tartness that quenches,
not orange.

Oranges would not surrender so easily.
I watched my father to see it done.
He would bite the bitter end,
or force back an opening with the side of a spoon.
Once cracked,
fingers pried
burrowing and pulling,
fighting grip of juicy pulp.
In the end,
the pieces of the shell
were big and few
and the fruit worth the price of any sting of small cuts.

Last night,
at the end of my fingers,
I saw my father's hands
open an orange.
Still a perfect gift.

I Didn't Know You

I didn't know you
except after death,
and for this I'm glad
because now life won't
prove me wrong
when I try to remember
what you ought to have been.

Let's let that be for now,
you, the product of my creation
and me, the product of yours.
Apart from us, we really don't exist,
unless someone else has remembering,
but from what I've seen,
the world forgets,
and then I'm no better
for opening my eyes and making
your life go.
Then I'm all that's left
and there's not enough to
fill the living for two that
must be in one.

Strange how life and death
follow patterns that can't
be followed by the eye,
but only by the forgetting
and the remembering.
And if forgotten,
we're dead.
Unless someone else can recall
the numbers of hair
and the living we kept in our minds.

"...healthy children will not fear life if their elders have integrity enough not to fear death."

—Erik Erikson, *Childhood and Society*

Crispus Attucks

Was Crispus Attucks a patriot?

We need to know.

Was he welcome here?
Then—when he took a musket ball—
or now,
as we breathe over the land he's buried under?

Was the transcontinental railroad
America's achievement—
stretched across native lands,
its length so decorated
with Asian, Irish, and formerly enslaved bones
above and below?

Magnum Opus

Growing up, my father did all the work around the house.
I was his apprentice as he wired outlets,
built stud walls, and focused timing lights
(when cars had carburetors).

Later, I went to college and grad school—
got extra letters to line up after my name on letterhead.
Those never help me when I'm crawling under the house
running duct work or a new water line.
Sometimes my friends think I'm more
homo habilis than *homo sapiens*
and they call me when their drains back up.
I'm no craftsman, but can still perform the magic of
turning kiln-dried
into end tables and bookcases and fence enclosures.

When I told my friends that I built my own casket,
they cringed and changed the subject.
"Really, it was a fun project"— I protest—
(they'll see the elegance if I explain.)
There's so much reverse engineering starting with
the dimensions of a concrete cemetery vault and
modified by my BMI.
Finished it with hinged lid— folding handles— varnished oak
and decoupage decorations as imperfect as I am.

Their only question:
"Where would you keep something like that?"

They're trying to point toward a flaw in my thinking,
but it doesn't work
I've got it worked out.

"It's hoisted on a skid I designed—
hanging from the rafters in my garage—
cranked to truss-level with a winch that makes an easy
up and down—

Wanna see?"

They never do.

Think it morbid.
That bothers me.
Do they think it impractical— as if *they'd* never need one?
But, if everything goes right, mine will be used.
My children and grandchildren will see me lying in it,
maybe even laughing at the amateurish skill that they learned
    to admire in me.

Covid Masking *

Who is that masked man?
a bystander asks
as the Lone Ranger rides off—
and "Heigh-ho Silver, away!"

A bystander asks
"Do we need any of this, at all?
and Heigh-ho Silver, away!"
but in the *away*, some are on life-support.

Do we need any of this at all?
These are neighbors I don't know,
but in the *away*, some are on life support
while I stare into my bathroom mirror.

These are neighbors I don't know,
as the Lone Ranger rides off—
I stare into my bathroom mirror—
Who is this masked man?

---

*A pantoum: a poem of any length, composed of four-line stanzas in which the second and fourth lines of each stanza serve as the first and third lines of the next stanza. The last line of a pantoum is often the same as the first.

Last Dance

I saw a man stop dancing.
It was at the bar and a band was playing,
a good band.
The regulars came to dance
and drink,
and laugh,
and make up stories
that got bigger
with the amplified beat of the bass guitar.
An older man was there,
not much older.

He had come to dance

All in black,
two-tone shoes,
silver buckle
he had the moves.
He and his partner did not miss a step
until he just stopped.
Would have gone down hard
but for the woman in his arms
who gently floated at his side.
Dance floor suddenly clear
and the squad repeating
"Clear."
Three times they shocked him
before sliding him onto a body board,
gurneying him out the door

He had come to dance.

Thanksgiving Parade

My ears
were not ready when
the marching band
hit a blaring
downbeat.
The tune was
"Simple Gifts," now
tempoed for a
march
as if
an army of pacifists
had taken
a sudden
militant turn.
Such a plain tune
fully ornamented
rising above
all heads
and still upward,
up to where
Garfield and Snoopy
romped
to break free
from the puny
humans straining
on string leashes.
At the sound,
all the dead Shakers
began to roll.

OUR BIRCHES
(With apologies to Robert Frost)

Thin and small when we
peeled burlap
from root ball,
it grew straight and tall.
I grew, too,
but older–not taller,
no longer tempted to climb
dark branches
until the trunks dipped
me back to earth.
Nearby,
the lake fends off ice storms,
shaping weather to suit its
moods of rain or snow.
Ice fog is a different thing,
but rare,
so our trees remain
unconquered
fearing neither
boy nor ice–
stretching toward sky's inner dome,
not to shatter,
but to brush against like a cat grown familiar
and straining to garner affection
from some outstretched hand.

Epitaph

Life is a stack of choices
piled in the clutter of everyday.
Some I made,
some not,
and
one day choices will be done.
Until then,
I am here.

ABOUT THE AUTHOR

Rob Smith believes that poetry is the most personal form of writing. After reviewing his body of work, he compiled *Eyes on Mars* as a poetic memoir based on childhood memories of how three young children, left on their own, managed to create a safe place located just under the radar of adult supervision.

Growing up as the middle child of a working class family in Youngstown, Ohio, his world was thrown into chaos at the death of his young mother. Her loss threatened to shatter the bonds between siblings until their father resolved to try to stitch a household back together. Parallel to his father's efforts, three children created their own new reality as a mechanism for coping.

After a career as a Presbyterian minister and university instructor, Rob returned to Ohio where he enjoys the life of a writer near the shores of Lake Erie.

He is the author of eight novels, but has also received recognition for poetry. In 2006 he won the Robert Frost Poetry Award given by the Frost Foundation in Lawrence, MA. He holds his undergraduate degree from Westminster College in Pennsylvania and master and doctoral degrees from Princeton Theological Seminary. *Eyes on Mars* is his fourth book of poetry.

Visit: SmithWrite.net

PHOTO CREDIT: Al Freeman

Aknowledgements

Writing is a solitary experience. Poets and novelists must go into themselves to create something that expresses their innermost world of thought. The next (and sometimes most frightening) step is that moment when the writing is shared and becomes a matter for public discussion.

Every new author that I've known tells of the feelings of vulnerability which accompany the first time that their book or poem is set free into the world. Thankfully, I have found a company of partners to assuage the anxiety. For nearly twenty years, Nancy Brady has been my editor. She has spent many hours reading and rereading, making suggestions, or demanding rewrites. She even made me face the dreaded ⅄ (awkward). Editors are a writer's best friend in that they work very hard to make us look good.

Finally, I am grateful to Dr. Heather Demos and the Huron Family Eye Care Center. She has kept her eyes on my retinas while I've been thinking about Mars.

RBS, 2024

The following poems were first published by in 2008 by Bird Dog Publishing in a volume entitled *256 Zones of Gray*: "Red Huffy," "Watching," "I Remember Her Much Taller," "Fear," "My Last Walk," "I Didn't Know You," "Groundhog," and "Last Dance."

"Sister," "Tangerines, Easy to Peel," and "Thanksgiving Parade" first appeared in *The Immigrant's House* (Drinian Press, 2012).

www.ingramcontent.com/pod-product-compliance
Lightning Source LLC
Chambersburg PA
CBHW020950090426
42736CB00010B/1345